My Rustic Sandwiches

My Rustic Sandwiches

Great Recipes to Savor Artisan Bread

Sam Sidawi

Daniel's Rustic Bread

Montreal

First published in Canada in 2009
by Daniel's Rustic Bread
3484 Sources Blvd. Suite 423
Dollard-Des-Ormeaux, QC H9B 1Z9
www.danielsrusticbread.com

10 9 8 7 6 5 4 3 2 1

Text, design and photography
© Sam Sidawi 2009

ISBN: 978-0-9812935-0-9

A catalog record is available from
Library and Archives Canada

Printed in Lebanon

CONTENTS

Introduction

Food always tastes better when it is enjoyed with others, so as a food and artisan bread lover I want to share with you some of the great sandwiches that I have had. With my artisan bread making DVDs which some of you may already have, I was able to share my knowledge on how to make great bread. I am grateful to so many bread enthusiasts who sent me nice emails over the years expressing the rewarding feeling that they got after successfully baking their first loaf of bread.

Although this book is mainly about sandwich ideas, you will find a section about artisan bread along with recipes on different breads. A great sandwich starts with great bread. You can stuff the sandwich with so many different ingredients but if the bread has no flavor and texture the sandwich may taste good but not great.

Bread making is a nice and rewarding craft because it satisfies most of our senses. First you get to make it with your own hands, then watch it turn into a nice golden loaf. While it's baking you smell the nice aroma and when you eat it you enjoy the great taste and texture. Of course you can still enjoy great bread if you buy it at an artisan bakery but for those of you who don't have such bakeries in your neighborhood, making your own bread might be a nice hobby to pick up.

Finally I would like to point out that for those of you who would like to learn how to make bread you can use some of the formulas provided in this book, however bread making is a craft and sometimes a recipe may not be enough to learn how to make great bread. The recipes in this book are a good start but to fully understand the different steps of bread making, I suggest watching a DVD where you can see the process and be able to follow it visually step by step. You will then be able to replicate the process in your home and produce first class artisan bread. You can order my bread making DVDs online at: Daniel's Rustic Bread: www.danielsrusticbread.com.

For those of you who simply want to explore fun & savory sandwiches you will find great ideas and recipes in this book for all tastes.

Artisan Bread

Handcrafted loaves of bread that are full of flavor when you smell them, hearty looking and somewhat rustic with a deep golden crispy crust and a soft airy crumb and a very distinct taste and texture, is one way to describe artisan bread.

Artisan bread is also bread that doesn't stay fresh for too long because it is made without chemicals and preservative using only water, unbleached flour, salt and yeast. Sourdough bread is made without commercial yeast using a starter made naturally with flour, water and wild yeast that is present in the air. Artisan bread can also contain a pinch of ascorbic acid (Vitamin C) to stimulate the yeast and some malted barley flour which is a yeast food that also helps develop the fermentation process.

Handcrafted artisan bread does not necessarily have to be kneaded by hand. An electric mixer can be used which does a good job, however the dividing, shaping and the handling of the dough has to be done by hand specially the shaping because machines deflate the air/gas inside the dough and that air consists of the uneven holes that are in the crumb which give the bread flavor and an open airy texture. Tap the loaf of artisan bread on the bottom and you should hear a hollow sound which is a sign that the bread is not dense. Artisan bread is also baked on a stone which distributes the heat evenly and absorbs the extra moisture in the dough giving the loaves a crispy crust.

The most important part after you have examined the bread is the taste. After all we're making bread so we can eat it. Artisan bread is full of flavor and ranges in taste depending on the kind, from mild and somewhat sweet to tangy and sour with lots of texture. After all whichever kind you are eating, it is all about the flavor and wonderful aroma that it leaves in your mouth. Enjoying great bread is not only eating, it's an experience.

About Flour

There are two kinds of white flour that are good for bread making, all purpose flour and bread flour. The difference between the two is that bread flour has higher gluten. Gluten is the protein level in the flour which makes the dough extensible. High gluten flour makes the dough more elastic and allows it to stretch and rise more. High gluten flour is not necessarily better for bread, certain bread like French baguette is made with medium gluten flour and other bread like whole grain is made with higher gluten flour.

All purpose flour, French & Italian flour

The white all purpose flour that is most common has a medium gluten of about 11.5% to 11.7% of protein level versus the bread flour has about 12.5% protein level. Typical French flour has a medium gluten of about 11.6% protein level and is closest to all purpose flour in that regard, except French flour contains a higher amount of ash. Ash content in flour is the mineral content and it gives the bread a deeper golden color, a flakier crust and a somewhat nutty flavor. French flour is called "Style 55 flour" and it has been replicated by some flour mills in the US and Canada and it is called "French Style" flour. If you want to try to replicate French style flour, use 1 or 2 tablespoons of whole grain flour in your mix (whole wheat or rye) which will give a somewhat similar color and effect. Italian flour or "00" (double zero flour) has a lower gluten of about 9 or 10% and makes a very soft dough, that's why Italian bread recipes in the US and Canada require more water specially for Ciabatta to make a very soft dough. If you're using Italian flour reduce the amount of water in the recipe by about 15 to 20%.

Bread Flour

Bread flour is also good for bread making specially when mixing it with whole grain flour which contains bran that makes the dough harder to stretch and rise. That's why they make it special for bread machines, it handles tough kneading. I use it sometimes in country and multi grain bread. Bread flour will give a better rise and volume for the dough but it makes the bread more chewy, that's why I use all purpose or French style flour for baguettes because I don't like crusty bread that is too chewy. You can experiment with both all purpose and bread flour and mix half & half or percentages to tailor it to your preferences.

Unbleached Flour

It's preferable to use unbleached flour when making bread. You don't want any chemicals in your flour. One good thing about making your own bread is that you control what goes in your mouth by choosing the best and safest ingredients available without preservative and chemicals.

Organic Flour

Organic flour is free of pesticides and herbicide and that's a good reason to use it when available. Some organic flour does not contain malted barley flour which is an ingredient that is available in most flour. Malted barley flour is a yeast food, it helps in the fermentation process. Check the ingredients in your flour, if it's not listed add a teaspoon to the mix. You can find malted barley flour or dough enhancer at the super market or specialty stores in the baking and flour section.

Filtered water

Another advantage of making your own bread is you can use filtered or bottled water that is free of chlorine and other unwanted particles that can change the taste of bread. Typically if you're making a batch of dough that weighs 2 lbs, you're only using 1 1/2 to 2 cups of water so it really doesn't cost much to use bottled water.

Yeast

There are 3 types of yeast and they all get the job done. *"Instant Yeast"*, *"Active Dry Yeast"* and *"Fresh Compressed Yeast"*. I use instant yeast and the recipes I provide are based on instant yeast. It's easier to use instant yeast because you can mix it directly with the flour without activating it with warm water first which is done with active dry yeast. Instant yeast also requires a lesser amount than active dry yeast. If you're using active dry yeast use 25% more than the recipe requires. Fresh compressed yeast is hard to find and store and is mostly available for commercial use, although a lot of bakers use instant yeast. If you're using fresh compressed yeast you will need 3 times the amount of instant yeast, so if the recipe requires 1 teaspoon or 1 ounce of instant yeast you want to use 3 teaspoons or 3 ounces of fresh compressed yeast.

Salt

Salt prevents the dough from rising too fast which limits oxidation. Oxidation is when the dough looses the flavor and taste.

Pre-ferment

A pre-ferment is a dough or a batter like mixture of water, flour and yeast that is used with the final dough to improve the texture, character and flavor of the bread. It can simply be a French bread dough that is mixed with another batch of French dough which is what is called old dough mixed with new dough. The old dough in this case is the pre-ferment and is called *Pâte fermentée* and means fermented dough. Another kind of pre-ferment is the *Poolish* which is more like a soft batter rather than dough. It is easy to make and performs very well with baguettes and is the standard today in France for making baguettes. It is called *Poolish* because the French learned it from the Polish and named it after them. The Italian version of pre-ferment is called *Biga* and it's like *Pâte fermentée* except it does not contain salt.

Autolyse

In the initial stage of mixing, when the water is fully absorbed by the flour, the dough is left to rest for about 20 minutes before continuing the mixing cycle. This resting period is called *Autolyse*, it relaxes the dough and makes it softer, more extensible and easier to knead. It also decreases the time of mixing which can prevent the dough from oxidizing.

Retarding the proofing

Proofing is the last fermentation step that is done after the shaping. To manipulate time, some bakers retard the proofing by putting the dough in the refrigerator for several hours or overnight which allows the dough to proof very slowly at a cold temperature. This process is done mainly for time manipulation to allow the bread to be baked at a later time or the following morning. Retarding can develop more flavor to the bread due to the slow fermentation, however it can form air bubbles or blisters on the skin of the bread during baking which affects only the look of the bread and not the taste. If you plan to retard the proofing, after shaping your dough, place it on a baking pan lined with parchment paper, spray it lightly with oil, cover it with plastic wrap and put it in the refrigerator. Remove the dough from the refrigerator about 30 minutes before you bake.

The 12 steps of bread making

1- **Scaling:** Preparing and scaling ingredients.

2- **Mixing:** Kneading & developing the gluten to allow the dough to stretch and rise.

3- **Fermenting:** Allowing the dough to ferment and rise to develop flavor.

4- **Folding:** Folding the dough during fermentation to redistribute the yeast.

5- **Dividing:** Dividing the dough and scaling it to final weight.

6- **Pre-Shaping:** Rough shaping of the dough.

7- **Bench Resting:** Allowing the pre-shaped dough to rest for about 20 minutes to be more extensible for further shaping like baguettes (this step is not necessary for round loaves or *batards* (oval loaves) because they don't require further shaping.)

8- **Shaping:** Finalizing the shaping into baguettes or other shapes.

9- **Proofing:** Second fermentation which allows the dough to rise and develop more.

10- **Scoring:** Slashing the dough with a blade to allow it to expand during baking.

11- **Baking:** Or hearth baking which means baking on a stone deck oven.

12- **Cooling:** While cooling, the bread is still developing and cooking inside. It is important not to cut right into it when it comes out of the oven. Allow 30 to 45 minutes for small to medium loaves and an hour or more for bigger loaves.

Baker's Math

The percentage formula in the following recipes is based on the total weight of flour which is always at 100%. All other ingredients are a percentage of that weight. Once you determine the weight of the flour it is easy to figure out the weight of the other ingredients by applying the percentage in the formula.

- To use the percentage formula to make any desired amount of bread, for example 2 lbs. First you have to determine the weight of the flour needed to make 2 lbs of bread. Add all percentages in the formula to get the Total Percentage (Total%) which is 250.65 % or 2.5065 in the baguettes final dough formula (See the baguettes recipe).

- Next you divide the weight of the bread you want to make by the Total Percentage:
2 lbs ÷ 2.5065 = 0.79 lbs or 12.64 ounces of flour.
Now that you have the flour weight needed to make 2 lbs of bread you can apply the percentage formula to determine the weight of water which is 47% of 12.64 = 5.94 ounces. The same applies to salt, yeast and poolish.

- Use the same method to determine the flour weight in the poolish using the poolish Total Percentage.

Approximate weights & measurements

1 cup flour = 4.5 oz
1 cup water/milk/oil = 8 oz
1 teaspoon instant yeast = 0.1 oz
1 teaspoon salt = 0.25 oz
1 cup dough/poolish/pâte fermentée/biga/sourdough starter = 7 oz
1 tablespoon oil/butter = 0.5 oz
1 tablespoon honey / molasses = 0.66 oz
1 tablespoon sugar = 0.5 oz

1 oz = 28 grams
350° Fahrenheit = 176° Celsius
450° Fahrenheit = 233° Celsius
500° Fahrenheit = 260° Celsius

1 fluid oz = 29 milliliter
tsp = Teaspoon
tbsp = Tablespoon
1 lb = 0.45 kg (450 grams)

Baguettes with Poolish

Makes 4 baguettes about 14 inch long

Poolish	Volume	Weight	% Formula*
Flour	1 1/2 cups	7 oz	100 %
Water	3/4 cup + 3 tbsp	7.4 oz	105 %
Instant Yeast	1/16 tsp (pinch)	0.01 oz	0.1 %
			(Total % 205.1)

Final Dough	Volume	Weight	% Formula*
Flour	3 1/4 cups	14.4 oz	100 %
Water	3/4 cup	6.7 oz	47 %
Instant Yeast	1 tsp	0.1 oz	0.65 %
Salt	1 3/4 tsp	0.4 oz	3 %
Poolish	2 cups (all above)	14.4 oz	100 %
Ascorbic acid**	pinch	pinch	pinch
(optional)			(Total % 250.65)

Poolish:

Mix flour water & yeast in a bowl with a spoon until all water is absorbed. Cover the bowl with plastic wrap overnight or up to 18 hours at room temperature. Poolish can be refrigerated for 2 to 3 days after 4 to 5 hours at room temperature.

Final Dough:

1- Scale dry ingredients (flour salt & yeast) in a bowl. Place salt and yeast apart from each other in the bowl.

2- Mix dry ingredients with a whisker then add water & Poolish and mix for 1 minute with the paddle if using an electric mixer, or a spoon if mixing by hand to form into one ball. Cover the bowl with a cloth and let it rest for 20 minutes (Autolyse: See pg 10). After the resting period, mix for 4 minutes using a dough hook on first speed then mix for an additional 3 to 4 minutes on second speed, and an additional minute if necessary on third speed. If mixing by hand knead for about 12 to 17 minutes until the dough becomes elastic. Form the dough into a tight ball, lightly spray the bowl with oil and place the dough ball in it and roll it around to coat it with the oil. Cover the bowl with plastic wrap.

3- Ferment for 1 hour at room temperature (ideally at 78° Fahrenheit. If your kitchen temperature is cool then ferment for 15 or 20 minutes longer or use warm water when mixing the dough).

4- Lightly fold the dough by gently punching it down and reshaping it into a ball without deflating it too much. Cover the bowl again and continue fermenting for another hour.

5- Divide the dough into 4 pieces on a lightly floured surface using a dough divider or a scraper.

6- Pre-shape the dough into balls or oblong shape gently and cover them with a damp cloth to keep the skin humid.

7- Let the dough rest 20 to 30 minutes (bench resting, see pg 11).

8- Tap the dough balls with your hand by gently flattening them then fold them like a letter from each side and seal to form into an oval loaf. Tap the dough and flatten it again and fold from one end into the other end and seal it again with your finger and the heal of your hand to form it into a tight oval shape (tightening the surface makes the dough rise in a round shape). Place your hands in the center of the loaf and roll out by stretching the dough into a long thin round baguette about 13 to 14 inch long. Place the baguettes on a couche (canvas cloth, see picture below) and cover them with a damp cloth.

9- Transfer the baguettes onto a peel or the back of a baking pan lined with parchment paper. Use a long piece of wood board to transfer the baguettes from the counter to the peel by lifting the couche and flipping the baguettes onto the board, then flip the baguettes over again onto the peel or the pan.

10- Score the dough with a blade or a sharp knife by slashing it without putting pressure or weight on the dough.

11- Slide the dough into the oven stone and bake at 445° Fahrenheit for about 27 minutes. For a darker color bake 5 to 7 more minutes.

12- Remove the bread from the oven and cool for at least 20 minutes before you serve.

Note: For shaping a pan loaf and free standing loaves "Boule" and "Batard" see shaping in "Whole Grain Recipe", pg18.

* % Formula: The percentage formula is based on weight only, not volume.

** Ascorbic Acid is vitamin C and it helps stimulate the yeast. A very small amount is used and the weight is negligent, that's why we note "pinch" even in bigger commercial batches.

• Most flour contains malted barley flour which is a yeast food except in some organic flour. Check ingredients, if it's not listed add a teaspoon to the mix.

Suggestion:

For detailed and visual step by step instructions you can order my DVD on Baguettes & French Bread online at:
Daniel's Rustic Bread - www.danielsrusticbread.com

The final results should be a nice golden brown crispy crust and a light crumb with irregular holes and an off white color.

Baker's Couche is a canvas cloth made with untreated natural fiber used to proof (ferment) the dough. The rough surface absorbs the extra moisture in the dough giving the bread a thick crispy crust. You can order the couche online at: www.danielsrusticbread.com

Ciabatta with Biga

Biga	Volume	Weight	% Formula*
Flour	2 3/4 cups	12.5 oz	100 %
Instant Yeast	3/4 tsp	0.07 oz	0.6 %
Water	1 cup	8.25 oz	66 %
			(Total % 166.6)

Final Dough	Volume	Weight	% Formula*
Flour	2 3/4 cups	12.5 oz	100%
Instant Yeast	2 3/4 tsp	0.28 oz	2.25 %
Salt	2 tsp	0.5 oz	4 %
Water	1 1/4 cup	10 oz	80 %
Biga	(all above)	21 oz	167 %
Ascorbic acid	pinch	pinch	pinch
(optional)			(Total % 353.25)

Biga:
1- Mix flour & yeast, add water and mix for 1 minute to collect ingredients into one ball.
2- Mix for 4 to 5 minutes using a dough hook on 1st speed if using an electric mixer and an additional 40 to 50 seconds on 2nd speed (if mixing by hand knead for 6 to 10 minutes until the dough is elastic and smooth).
3- Form the dough into a ball, place it in an oiled bowl, cover the bowl with plastic wrap and ferment for 1 hour.
4- Lightly fold the dough by gently punching it down and reshaping it into a ball without deflating it too much. Cover the bowl again and continue fermenting for another hour.

Ciabatta Final Dough:
1- Scale flour salt & yeast in a bowl. Place salt and yeast apart from each other in the bowl.
2- Mix dry ingredients, add water, biga & ascorbic acid and mix for 1 minute to collect ingredients into one ball. Mix for 2 to 3 minutes using a dough hook if using an electric mixer (If mixing by hand knead for 6 to 7 minutes). Mix for another 3 to 5 minutes on second speed (if mixing by hand mix for 6 to 8 minutes). Mix for an additional 30 to 50 seconds on 3rd speed if needed until dough is elastic and smooth.
3- Sprinkle the counter generously with flour as the dough will be very wet and sticky. Transfer the dough to the counter (if the dough sticks to the counter scrape it with a dough scraper). Divide the dough into 2 pieces using a scraper, form them into rough squares, stretch them into long rectangles about 6 inch wide by 15 inch long, sprinkle flour on top of the dough and cover it with a cloth.

4- Ferment the dough for 30 minutes.

5- Fold the dough gently like a letter into rough squares, stretch them again into rectangles & ferment for an additional 30 to 40 minutes. The stretching allows the gluten to develop more and will form the large irregular holes in the crumb.

6- Place the dough rectangles on parchment paper, stretch them a bit more, dust them with flour, cover them with a damp cloth and proof for about 90 minutes.

7- Transfer the dough to a peel or the back of a pan by sliding the parchment paper onto the peel or the pan, then slide it into the oven & bake for 25 to 30 minutes at 450° Fahrenheit.

8- Remove the bread from the oven and cool for 30 minutes.

* % Formula: The percentage formula is based on weight only, not volume.

Suggestion:

For detailed and visual step by step instructions you can order my DVD on Ciabatta bread online at:
Daniel's Rustic Bread - www.danielsrusticbread.com

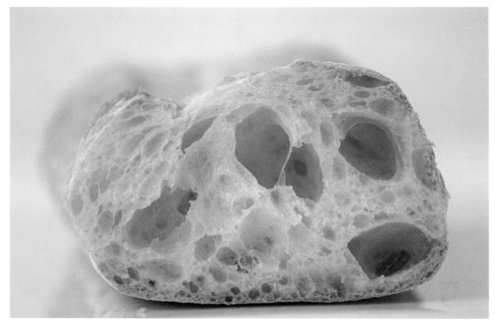

The wet dough and the stretching make
large irregular holes in the crumb.

Focaccia

Dough	Volume	Weight	% Formula*
Flour	4 cups	18 oz	100 %
Instant Yeast	3/4 tsp	0.075 oz	0.42 %
Salt	1 1/4 tsp	0.32 oz	1.8 %
Water	1 1/2 cups	12 oz	67 %
Olive Oil	2 tbsp	1 oz	6 %

(Total % 175.22)*

1- Scale flour, salt & yeast in a bowl. Place salt and yeast apart from each other in the bowl.

2- Add liquids to dry ingredients and mix for 1 minute with a paddle if using an electric mixer, or a spoon if mixing by hand to form into one piece. Cover the bowl with a cloth and let it rest for 15 minutes. After the resting period, mix for 3 minutes using a dough hook on first speed then mix for an additional 3 to 4 minutes on second speed, and an additional minute on third speed. If mixing by hand knead for about 15 minutes.

3- Place the dough in a lightly oiled bowl, cover and ferment for 1 1/2 to 2 hours.

4- Drizzle some olive oil on a baking pan and place the dough on it. Drizzle some more olive oil on the dough and stretch it with your hands by pressing with your fingers on it until it fills the pan or becomes a bit thinner than half inch thick. Sprinkle your favorite herbs or toppings like rosemary and olives and cover with plastic wrap.

5- Proof for 45 minutes and bake in the middle rack at 450° Fahrenheit for about 25 minutes or until it slightly browns.

* % Formula: The percentage formula is based on weight only, not volume.

Pizza: This recipe is also good for pizza dough. After step 3, divide the dough and form it into 4 balls. Cover the balls with plastic wrap and proof them for 45 minutes, then stretch them into 10 inch round circles. Add toppings and bake on the bottom rack on a pizza stone at 500° F for 7 to 8 minutes.

Suggestion:
For detailed and visual step by step instructions
you can order my DVD on Focaccia & Pizza online at:
Daniel's Rustic Bread - www.danielsrusticbread.com

Whole Grain

Final Dough	Volume	Weight	% Formula*
Flour	5 cups	23 oz	100 %
Instant Yeast	2 3/4 tsp	0.28 oz	1.25 %
Salt	1 3/4 tsp	0.46 oz	2 %
Dough Enhancer	4 1/2 tsp	0.46 oz	2 %
Water	1 cup	8 oz	35 %
Milk	1 cup	8 oz	35 %
Vegetable Oil	1 3/4 tbsp	0.92 oz	4 %
Honey/Molasses	1 1/3 tbsp	0.92 oz	4 %

Total % 183.25*

- **Whole wheat:** Use 100% whole wheat flour.
- **Multigrain:** Use 2 cups of multigrain mix like 7 or 9 grain and 3 cups of white flour. Add 2 tablespoons of seeds (flax, sunflower, sesame, poppy, mullet...) in the mix, and 2 tablespoons on top of the crust after the shaping.
- **Rye:** Use 1 3/4 cups whole rye flour and 3 1/4 cups white bread flour. Add 2 teaspoons caraway seeds in the flour.

1- Scale dry ingredients in a bowl. Place salt and yeast apart from each other in the bowl.

2- Add liquids to dry ingredients and mix for 1 minute with a paddle if using an electric mixer, or a spoon if mixing by hand to form into one ball. Cover the dough with a cloth and let it rest for 20 to 30 minutes. After the resting period, mix for 3 minutes using a dough hook on first speed then mix for an additional 4 minutes on second speed, and an additional minute on third speed. If mixing by hand knead for 15 to 18 minutes.

3- Place the dough in a lightly oiled bowl, cover and ferment for 1 to 1 1/2 hours.

4- Shape the dough into desired form. For a pan loaf, transfer the dough onto a lightly floured surface, flatten it gently into a square the same width as the loaf pan. Roll the square to form a log, seal the seam and place it in a lightly oiled pan. Cover the pan with a damp cloth. To make a round "boule", fold the dough gently with your hands into a round ball and seal the seam well and place it in a round basket lined with a couche seam side up. To make an oval "batard", tap the dough gently by flattening it a bit and fold it like a letter and seal the seam well and place it in an oval basket lined with a couche seam side up. See page 19.

5- Proof for 1 to 1 1/2 hours. For the multigrain bread, mist the dough with water and sprinkle 2 tablespoons of seeds.

6- Score the dough with a blade. For pan loaf scoring is optional. For the boule and batard, first transfer the dough by flipping the basket over onto a peel lined with parchment paper then score it.

7- Bake the pan loaf in a pre-heated oven at 350° Fahrenheit for 45 to 50 minutes. For the boule and batard, slide them onto the baking stone inside the pre-heated oven and bake at 425 degrees Fahrenheit for 45 to 50 minutes.

8- Remove the pan loaf from the pan right away after baking and place it on a cooling rack for about 1 hour.

* % Formula: The percentage formula is based on weight only, not volume.

Suggestion:

For detailed and visual step by step instructions you can order my DVD on whole grain bread online at: Daniel's Rustic Bread - www.danielsrusticbread.com

Proofing free standing loaves, "Boule" and "Batard"

Simple & Savory

Camembert Cheese on Baguette

Sometimes keeping it simple allows the flavor of the bread to stand out. Cheese is a great way to enjoy bread and makes a great snack. I often enjoy a strong tasting Camembert cheese on a crusty baguette in the morning and other times I like a more subtle tasting cheese like Swiss Emmentaler or Gruyère.

D'Iberville

D'Iberville is a strong flavorful semi soft cheese made in Quebec. When you buy cheese always smell it, if you like it strong it should smell pungent and if you like it mild it should not have much smell like Brie or young Camembert.

Herbed Goat Cheese on Ciabatta

This soft somewhat pungent cheese is light and sometimes comes crusted with peppercorn or just plain.

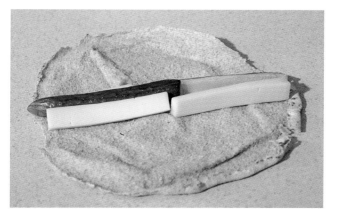

For a change I also like to snack on Kashkaval cheese and pita bread. Kashkaval is made with sheep's milk and imported from Bulgaria, Greece or other neighboring countries famous for this cheese. It has a somewhat strong taste but at the same time smooth with a very distinct flavor. It's great with any bread, try it on pita with cucumber like they eat it in the eastern Mediterranean region.

Lebneh is a typical Lebanese creamy cheese made out of plain yogurt. It's eaten mostly for breakfast with olives, cucumber, olive oil and dry or fresh mint. It's very easy to make, simply strain a medium container of plain yogurt (2 lbs) in a strainer lined with cheese cloth for a few hours or overnight, add half a teaspoon of salt, mix it and it's ready to serve. Already made Lebneh can be found at some super markets and ethnic stores.

Blue Cheese on Baguette

Goes well with crusty bread. The three kinds that are most popular are the French Roquefort which is the strongest, Italian Gorgonzola, a bit milder, and English blue cheese, a bit creamier and very flavorful.

Fresh Mozzarella, Balsamic Vinegar, Tomato, Grilled Red Pepper and Fresh Basil on Ciabatta

The wet rustic dough gives this bread a nice open crumb with large irregular holes. Generously dusted with flour before baking to prevent the wet dough from sticking to hands and surfaces.

Feta Cheese, Tomato, Cucumber and Olive Oil on French Loaf Bread

Many countries now have their own version of Feta cheese. The most popular are Greek, Bulgarian is the saltiest but very strong and flavorful, and French has a more balanced saltiness.

Pâté

Pâtés and Terrines go very nicely with bread too. The most famous ones are "pâté de foie gras" made with goose liver.

Veggie on French Country Mini Batard

French country bread uses a small amount of whole rye flour which gives it a bit more flavor and a darker crust and crumb. Batard is an oval loaf of bread, it also means bastard in French.

Two batards attached to each other are called "Pain Fesse" which means "butt bread"... Well this one at least we know why but batard remains a mystery.

Tuna, Capers, Dijon Mustard, and Tomato on Multigrain Bread

A lighter version of the classic tuna salad sandwich. Also good on rye bread. Always a nice quick snack when time is not on your side.

Smoked Turkey, Avocado, Tomato
and Mayonnaise on Nine Grain Bread

Mortadella, Salami, Capicollo, Pepperoncini
and Mustard on Country Bread

Black Forest Ham, Red Leaf Lettuce, Tomato and Strong Mustard on Baguette

A classic all dressed ham sandwich.

Toasted Ham and Gruyère Cheese

Toasted Kashkaval Cheese and Tomato on Whole Wheat Pita Bread

Sautéed Dandelion, Caramelized Onions, Shaved Radish and a Squeeze of Lemon Juice on Pita Bread

Light, tasty and healthy. One of those feel good about yourself sandwiches.

Cut out the stems of the dandelion leaving about 2 inches on. Chop dandelion into 3 inches long, wash well and boil in water for 5 to 10 minutes (the boiling will take away some of the bitterness). Cool them with cold water and squeeze them tight with your hand to get most of the water out. Sauté the onions in olive oil on medium heat for about 20 minutes stirring them every 5 minutes until golden brown and place them on a plate lined with paper napkins to absorb the extra oil. Sauté the dandelion in the same oil for 7 to 10 minutes until they're soft salting them to taste. Spread the dandelion on a large plate to cool to room temperature, squeeze lemon juice and top with caramelized onions and shaved radish.

Suggestion: The dandelion will substantially reduce in size when cooked so make sure you get 2 large bunches or 4 smaller ones.

2 large bunches dandelion

2 tablespoons olive oil

2 onions, thinly sliced

1 handful shaved radish

Pinch of salt to taste

Juice of 2 lemons

Makes 4 sandwiches

Stuffed Country Boule with Grilled Eggplant, Zucchini, Red, Green and Yellow Pepper, Assorted Cold Cuts, Fresh Mozzarella and Watercress

A hearty colorful sandwich, great for a casual party. How do you eat it? You'll find your way...

Cut the eggplant and zucchini into 1/4 inch slices. Cut each pepper into 4 pieces removing the seeds. Place the vegetables on a pan, salt and pepper and drizzle olive oil to coat them and place them on the grill 7 to 10 minutes on each side. Peel the skin off the peppers, squeeze lemon juice on the vegetables and cool in the fridge for 20 minutes.

Open the boule from the top by slicing the top off and remove the crumb from the inside. Lightly butter the interior of the boule and stuff it in layers of vegetables and cold cuts one kind per layer. About half way through put a layer of mozzarella and keep stuffing it with the vegetables and cold cuts to the top. Place some watercress on the top and close the boule with the top sliced piece of bread. Place the boule on a plate, cover with plastic wrap and put in the fridge for about an hour to let the bread absorb the flavors and make the vegetables firm up a bit for better slicing.

The boule can stay in the fridge for several hours or overnight. When slicing the boule into sandwiches make sure to use a bread knife and cut into wedges by holding the top firmly and making sure the stuffing does not spill out.

Suggestion: You can broil the vegetables in the oven for about 30 minutes on high heat

3 peppers, red, green & yellow

1 large eggplant

2 zucchinis

1 lb assorted cold cuts
(Ham, salami, pepperoni)

6 slices fresh mozzarella

1 handful of watercress

Juice of half a lemon

Salt & pepper to taste

4 tablespoons olive oil

1 country boule

Makes 8 sandwiches

Hot & Gourmet

Sesame Crusted Grilled Salmon, Wasabe Mayonnaise, Red Onion and Tomato on Rustic Bread

Grilled on a wood plank for smoky flavor. If you're not crazy about salmon this dish will change your mind. I sometimes eat it as is without the bread and the next day I make the leftovers into sandwiches.

The wood plank is usually found at the super market in the fish section. Start by soaking the plank in water about one hour before you grill the fish. Season the salmon with salt and pepper then crust it with sesame. Fire up the barbecue and let it heat for five minutes on medium low heat. Remove the plank from the water and place the salmon on it and place on the grill. Cover the grill and cook for 25 to 30 minutes and serve.

Wasabe Mayonnaise: See "Spreads & Dips" section.

Suggestion: You can also broil the salmon in the oven but do not use the wood plank. Place it in a pan, drizzle a bit of olive oil and cook for 25 to 30 minutes at 400 degrees Fahrenheit.

Side dish: Roasted potatoes in herbs.

1 filet of salmon about 12 inches long

1 handful of black & white sesame

Salt & Pepper to taste

2 Tomatoes, sliced

1/2 red onion, sliced

1 teaspoon wasabe

1/3 cup mayonnaise

Makes 4 sandwiches

Sesame Crusted Grilled Salmon, Lemon Basil Mayonnaise, Diced Red Onions, Tomatoes and Parsley on Parisienne

Parisienne is a larger version of a baguette. It is usually the same length but twice as wide. It's great for sandwiches, the extra width gives more room to fit all the goodies.

Cook the salmon the same way as the previous dish. Chop the red onions, tomatoes and parsley into quarter inch pieces. Drizzle some lemon basil mayonnaise on bread, place chopped tomatoes and onions on the bread then top it with chunks of salmon and drizzle more lemon basil mayonnaise on top of the salmon and serve.

Lemon Basil Mayonnaise: Blend the mayonnaise, basil, mustard and lemon juice in a food processor to form a liquid dressing.

1 filet of salmon about 12 inches long

1 handful of Black & white sesame

Salt & Pepper to taste

2 Tomatoes, diced

1/2 red onion, diced

3 tablespoons chopped parsley

1 Parisienne cut into 4 pieces

Makes 4 sandwiches

Lemon basil mayonnaise

1 teaspoon strong mustard

1/3 cup mayonnaise

1 large bunch fresh basil

Juice of half a lemon

Seared Tuna, Sautéed Scallions and Ginger, Strong Mustard on Kaiser Bread

A soft light bread like kaiser is a good choice for seared fish because it doesn't overpower the delicate texture and flavor of the fish.

Cut the scallions lengthwise into thin strips (Julienne cuts), grate or mince the ginger and sauté in a tablespoon of olive oil for a minute. Add a tablespoon of soy sauce and sauté for an additional minute until scallions are a bit soft. Remove the ginger and scallions aside, season the tuna with salt & pepper and sear it in the same skillet on medium high heat for about one minute on each side. Spread strong mustard on the bread, place the tuna filet and top it with the scallions and ginger.

4 sushi grade tuna filets

1 tablespoon olive oil

1 tablespoon soy sauce

1 tablespoon grated ginger

2 scallions

4 kaiser rolls

Mustard to taste

Salt & pepper to taste

Makes 4 sandwiches

Mahi Mahi, Tartar Sauce and Lettuce on Sesame kaiser

My favorite meal when I'm in Hawaii is a Mahi fish sandwich. I specially like to have it at the small take away joints because they taste just as good as the ones served at fancy restaurants and I get to enjoy it out in the open. Not to mention that I get two sandwiches for the price of one compared to restaurants. In Hawaii this sandwich is served with just lettuce and tartar sauce on a hamburger bun or kaiser and I never want to change it.

Season the mahi filets with salt & pepper, grill or pan griddle 3 to 5 minutes on each side until well done. Spread some tartar sauce (see "Spreads & Dips" section) on the bread, put a lettuce and top it with the mahi and serve.

4 sandwich size mahi mahi filets

Tartar sauce to taste
(see "Spreads & Dips" section)

4 leaves of romaine lettuce

4 kaiser rolls

Salt & pepper to taste

Makes 4 sandwiches

Grilled Chicken, Roasted Garlic Mayonnaise, Roasted Tomatoes with Herbs, and Provolone Cheese on Ciabatta

Yummy ingredients, can't go wrong with this one!

Spread the tomato slices in a baking pan along with the garlic cloves skin on. Lightly drizzle some olive oil on top and a pinch of oregano or a mixture of Italian herbs. Bake for about 30 minutes at 375 degrees Fahrenheit. The Tomatoes may take an additional 5 to 10 minutes depending on their thickness.

Squeeze the garlic out of the skin by pinching one end, mash it with a fork and whisk it with the mayonnaise and place it in the fridge. Season the chicken with salt and pepper and grill on the barbecue 7 to 10 minutes on each side until well cooked. Cut open the Ciabatta rolls, spread the garlic mayonnaise on both pieces of bread, place few slices of roasted tomatoes followed by the chicken and a slice or two of provolone cheese and then put the sandwich back on the barbecue or in the oven for a couple of minutes to melt the cheese, and serve.

4 medium size boneless skinless chicken breasts

3 large tomatoes, sliced

4 garlic cloves, skin on

1/3 cup mayonnaise

1 teaspoon oregano

1 tablespoon olive oil

4 slices provolone cheese

4 ciabatta mini rolls

Makes 4 sandwiches

Side Dish: Roasted vegetables

Grilled Lamb Shoulder, Coarsely Cracked Pepper, Roasted Garlic and Parsley Mayonnaise, Radicchio, Tomato and Onion on Rosemary and Herbs Focaccia

This sandwich is loaded with flavors, can't get more Mediterranean than this.

Season the boneless Lamb shoulder with salt and coarsely cracked pepper and grill it on the barbecue 10 to 15 minutes on each side depending on how well done you like it. Slice the meat into half inch strips. Spread the roasted garlic & parsley mayonnaise on both pieces of bread, place few strips of meat on the bread followed by the tomato, onion, radicchio and serve.

2 lbs boneless lamb
shoulder or leg

2 tomatoes, sliced

1 onion, sliced

4 leaves of radicchio

1/3 cup roasted garlic &
parsley mayonnaise (see
"Spreads & Dips" section)

Makes 4 sandwiches

Rib Eye Roast in Red Wine Sauce with Shallots and Mushrooms on Baguette

A great dish to enjoy with family and friends during the holidays. You can eat it as a main dish and dip the bread in the sauce and the next day you can make the leftovers into sandwiches cold or hot.

5 lbs rib eye roast or a roast of your choice

1 1/2 lbs mushrooms

1 1/2 lbs shallots or small onions

1 bottle red wine

4 tablespoons flour

1 1/2 teaspoons salt

For rub

2 teaspoons fresh thyme

2 teaspoons rosemary

2 tablespoons olive oil

Salt & pepper to taste

3 baguettes

Makes 8 to 10 servings

Rub the roast all around with the olive oil, salt, pepper, rosemary and thyme and bake for 45 minutes at 375 degrees Fahrenheit until it starts browning a bit. Dissolve the flour and salt in the wine mixing them with a fork or a whisker and pour the wine on the roast (the flour will help thicken the sauce). Add the mushrooms and onions and bake for an additional 45 to 55 minutes.

Remove the pan from the oven, cover it with aluminum foil and let it rest for 20 minutes (It's important to let it rest so that the meat juices get absorbed by the meat). The meat will be medium and somewhat rosy on the inside. Cut the roast into about 1/4 inch slices and serve with the sauce, mushrooms and shallots.

If you like it well done bake for an additional 30 minutes. If you like it medium rare bake for 25 minutes less and take the meat out of the pan and cover it with foil while keeping the mushrooms, shallots and sauce in the oven to thicken for the remaining 25 minutes.

Suggestion: When you buy the roast, depending on the size, always ask the butcher about the suggested baking time.

Side Dish: Mashed potatoes

Burger au Poivre with Porteenie Mushroom on Sesame Kaiser Bread

Here's a burger kicked up a notch. This 3 color peppercorn sauce is typically made with steak but I've had this burger at a local restaurant and I found it pretty good except I added the mushroom which I thought gives it a bit of texture. Porteenie mushroom looks like portabella but a bit smaller.

Season the burgers with salt & some of the cracked peppercorn and grill them 3 to 4 minutes on each side until well done. Grill the mushrooms a couple of minutes on each side and serve with the burgers and the peppercorn sauce.

Peppercorn wine sauce: You can coarsely crack the peppercorn by placing them in a plastic bag and crushing them using the bottom of a pot, but I like to keep some of them as wholes. Melt the butter in a skillet over medium heat, sauté shallots until softened for about two minutes. Add the wine and the rest of the peppercorn and simmer stirring it for about two minutes. Add beef broth, cooking cream and simmer for three more minutes until sauce has thickened.

4 burger patties

4 kaiser rolls or burger buns

Salt to taste

Makes 4 sandwiches

Peppercorn sauce

2 tablespoons peppercorn

2 tablespoons butter

4 shallots, minced

1/2 cup red wine

1/2 cup beef broth

2 tablespoons cooking cream

Side Dish: French fries

Grilled Eggplant, Red Pepper, Zucchini, Red Onion with Goat Cheese and Balsamic Vinegar on Ciabatta

A classic Italian grilled vegetables sandwich.

Cut the eggplant and zucchini into 1/4 inch slices. Cut each red pepper into 4 pieces removing the seeds. Place the vegetables on a pan, salt and pepper and drizzle olive oil to coat them and place them on the grill 7 to 10 minutes on each side. Peel the skin off the peppers and drizzle some balsamic vinegar on the vegetables.

Place assorted vegetables on the bread and top it with goat cheese and serve.

Suggestion: You can broil the vegetables in the oven for about 30 minutes on high heat or until they start browning.

2 Italian eggplants

2 zucchinis

2 red bell peppers

1 red onion, thinly sliced

1 small package goat cheese

3 tablespoons olive oil

3 tablespoons balsamic vinegar

4 ciabatta mini rolls

Makes 4 sandwiches

Montreal's Smoked Meat on Rye Bread

To some it may taste like pastrami but to Montrealers it tastes like smoked meat. I can't remember the difference really because it's been a while since I've had the New York deli pastrami sandwich but I would have to eat both of them at the same time to really know the difference.

If you're baking rye bread using the recipe in this book you will notice that the bread is darker due to the use of whole rye flour instead of white rye flour.

Just yellow mustard and lots of smoked meat piled high.

Suggestion: Great with potato chips, coleslaw and pickles.

Grilled Chicken Ceasar Wrap with Shaved Parmesan Cheese

4 flour tortillas

4 medium boneless breasts of chicken

1 lettuce cut in 1 inch pieces

1/3 cup Caesar dressing

Shaved Parmesan cheese

Makes 4 wraps

1 lb finely ground meat

1/4 teaspoon salt

1/4 teaspoon all spice or pepper

1/4 teaspoon cinnamon

1/2 bunch of chopped parsley

1 medium onion, finely chopped

5 small pita bread

Makes 5 sandwiches

For the garnish

1 large white onion, thinly sliced

1/2 bunch of chopped parsley

1 large tomato, sliced

1 handful of pickled cucumber

1 cup hummus
(see "Spreads & Dips" section)

Kafta Kebab, White Onion, Parsley, Tomato, Hummus and Pickled Wild Cucumber on Pita Bread

Kafta is made with ground meat, onion, parsley and spices. It's a bit like hamburger but juicier and with more flavor.

Mix the ground meat, finely chopped onion, chopped parsley and spices with your hand like you're kneading dough then use a handful for each skewer and spread it on the skewer into about 5 inches long and 1 inch diameter. Grill on medium heat about 7 to 10 minutes on each side. Garnish the pita bread with hummus, chopped parsley, thinly sliced white onion, tomato, and pickled cucumber. Place the sandwich on the grill again a couple of minutes on each side to crisp the bread a bit leaving nice grill marks and serve.

Side Dish: Tabouleh salad

Side Dish: Tabouleh salad

Marinated Chicken Taouk, Pickled Turnip and Garlic Spread

If you love garlic this sandwich is the one.

Marinate the chicken for 3 to 6 hours in the fridge then put them on skewers and grill 7 to 10 minutes on each side. Garnish the bread with garlic spread & pickled turnip (see "Spreads & Dips" section) or pickled cucumber. Put the sandwich on the grill a couple of minutes on each side to crisp the bread a bit leaving nice grill marks and serve. Make sure not to overcook the chicken so that it stays juicy and tender.

Suggestion: Instead of marinated chicken you can also use regular barbecued chicken legs or breasts or roasted chicken. You can also use garlic mayonnaise instead of the garlic spread. Mash half a bulb of raw garlic in half a cup of mayonnaise.

Hold the lettuce: Some Middle Eastern fast food restaurants in North America may garnish this sandwich with lettuce and tomato. Make sure you say "Hold the lettuce" because it doesn't go well with this sandwich. Tomato is O. K. but it takes away from the intensity of the garlic. If you're a garlic lover keep it simple and lots of garlic.

1 lb chicken breasts cut into 2 inch pieces

Marinade

Juice of 2 small lemons

1/4 cup olive oil

1/4 cup plain yogurt

4 minced garlic cloves

Pinch of salt & Pepper

For the garnish

1/2 cup garlic spread
(see "Spreads & Dips" section)

1 handful of pickled turnip

4 to 5 small pita bread

Makes 4 to 5 sandwiches

Lamb Kebab, Grilled White Onion, Hummus and Pickled Cucumber

You can also use beef kebab or filet mignon.

1 lb lamb kebab or beef

Pinch of salt & pepper

1 large white onion cut in 4 wedges

4 to 5 pita bread

Makes 4 to 5 sandwiches

For the garnish

1 handful pickled cucumber

1 cup hummus
(see "Spreads & Dips" section)

Salt & pepper the meat. Put on skewers with chunks of white onion and grill 7 to 10 minutes on each side. Garnish the bread with hummus, grilled onion & pickled cucumber. Put the sandwiches on the grill a couple of minutes on each side to crisp the bread a bit leaving nice grill marks and serve.

Hold the lettuce: You can put tomato on this sandwich but no lettuce please! To me lettuce tastes terrible on a kebab sandwich but you can try it as long as you're the one eating it.

Pork Souvlaki, Tzatziki, Onion, Tomato on Greek Pita

Greek pita bread is thicker and does not have the pocket with two layers like the Middle Eastern pita. You can also make this sandwich with lamb shoulder or beef sirloin.

Marinate the meat for 3 hours or overnight in the fridge then put it on skewers and grill 7 to 10 minutes on each side. Grill the bread flat for few seconds and garnish with tzatziki (see "Spreads & Dips" section), tomato and onion.

2 lbs porc shoulder cut into cubes

Marinade

1/2 cup olive oil

Juice of 2 lemons

1 tablespoon red wine vinegar

4 minced garlic cloves

2 teaspoons dried or fresh oregano

1 teaspoon dried or fresh thyme

Makes 4 to 6 sandwiches

Beef Gyros, Tzatziki, Onion, Tomato on Greek Pita

This homemade version does not require a revolving skewer.

Mix ground beef, seasonings, garlic & onion and shape into 4 or 5 patties. Grill 3 to 4 minutes on each side until well done. Cut patties into thin slices. Grill the pita bread flat few seconds and garnish with tzatziki (see "Spreads & Dips" section), tomato, onion and top with a few slices of meat.

Side dish: Greek salad

1 1/2 lbs ground beef or lamb

1 1/2 teaspoons crushed oregano

2 minced garlic cloves

1 minced onion

Salt & pepper to taste

1 cup tzatziki
(see "Spreads & Dips" section

Makes 4 to 5 sandwiches

2 lbs beef sirloin cut into 1/4 inch strips

1 teaspoon salt

3/4 teaspoon each of black pepper, allspice, ground cardamom, cinnamon & nutmeg

1/4 cup olive oil

1/4 cup white or red vinegar

For the garnish

3 tomatoes cut into thick wedges

1 1/2 cups tahini sauce (See "Spreads & Dips" section)

1/2 bunch chopped parsley

1 medium white onion, thinly sliced

Makes 5 to 6 sandwiches

Shawarma, Tahini Sauce, Roasted Tomatoes, Parsley, Onions and Pickles on Pita

Typically this sandwich is made with meat that is high in fat and is shaved off a revolving skewer like the Greek Gyros. This homemade version is made with beef sirloin that is cut in 1/4 inch strips but you can use any meat cut you like.

Marinate the meat in the oil, vinegar and spices for few hours or overnight. Place the meat in a baking pan with the marinade. Place tomato wedges on top of the meat and bake in the oven at 425 degrees Fahrenheit for about 45 minutes or until the meat is well done. Mix the chopped parsley with the sliced onion and garnish the bread with it and top it with the meat, tomato, pickles and tahini sauce (See "Spreads & Dips" section).

Side dish: Fatouch or tabouleh salad

3/4 cup peeled fava beans

1/4 cup garbanzo beans

5 garlic cloves

1 onion

1/4 bunch cilantro

1 tablespoon parsley

1 teaspoon salt

1/4 teaspoon black pepper

1/4 teaspoon dry coriander

1/4 teaspoon cumin

1/4 teaspoon cinnamon

1/4 teaspoon baking soda

1/4 teaspoon baking powder

3 cups vegetable oil
(for frying)

For the garnish

1/2 bunch chopped parsley

2 tomatoes, sliced

1 handful pickles
(turnip or cucumber)

1 cup tahini sauce
(see "Spreads & Dips" section)

Makes 5 to 6 sandwiches

Falafel, Tahini Sauce, Tomato, Parsley, Pickled Turnip on Pita

This recipe is for making falafel from scratch but you can always find packaged falafel mix at super markets.

Soak the fava and garbanzo beans in water overnight. Drain the water from the beans and blend in a blender with onion, garlic, cilantro and parsley until finely ground. Add the rest of the seasonings, baking powder and baking soda and mix well with your hands as if you're kneading dough. Cover the mixture with a cloth and let it rest for about 40 minutes to an hour. After the resting you will notice the mixture has risen a bit, punch it down and mix it with your hand a bit and start forming small flat balls with your hand. You can also press the balls on a spoon to give a more round shape.

Fill a deep frying pan with about 2 inches of vegetable oil. Heat the oil and fry the falafel balls for few minutes until they brown. Garnish the pita bread with tomatoes, pickles, chopped parsley and tahini sauce (see "Spreads & Dips" section) and serve.

Side dish: Fatouch salad

Melty Delights

Stuffed Focaccia with Chorizo, Pancetta, Red, Yellow and Green Pepper, Sun-Dried Tomato Pesto and Mozzarella Cheese

Warm melty out of the oven stuffed focaccia. You can pick your favorite ingredients and mix and match.

In a pan sauté the chorizo, pancetta and peppers for about 15 to 20 minutes on medium heat until they brown a bit and the pancetta crisps a bit. Do not use any oil as the fat from the pancetta is enough to grease the pan. Divide the dough into 4 balls after the fermentation (after step 3 in Focaccia recipe, "Artisan Bread" section). Cover the dough balls with plastic wrap and let them rest for 30 minutes.

Stretch the dough balls into 7 by 12 inch rectangles about 1/4 inch thick. Lightly spread some sun dried tomato pesto in the middle of the dough followed by few tablespoons of the sautéed pancetta & peppers and top it with mozzarella cheese. Fold the dough like a letter, seal it well and cut it in half and place them in an oiled baking pan with open ends touching and lightly brush them with olive oil. Do the same for the 3 other dough balls and bake in the middle to high rack for 30 minutes at 440 degrees Fahrenheit or until they're nicely browned. See page 79 for more detailed instructions on stuffing & folding the dough.

Suggestion: You can also make panini grilled sandwiches with the same stuffing using French or Ciabatta bread slices.

1/2 cup chorizo, thinly sliced

1/2 cup diced pancetta

3 small different color peppers

1/2 cup sun dried tomato pesto

1/2 lb sliced mozzarella cheese

2 lbs focaccia dough
(see "Artisan Bread" section)

Makes 8 stuffed focaccias

Stuffed Mini Focaccia

You can also make the stuffed focaccia into small bite size rolls filling them with different kinds of ingredients, a good idea for sampling.

Follow the same instructions for the dough as the previous recipe. After folding the dough cut it into 1 inch pieces and place them on an oiled pan touching each other with no space in between. Bake the same way as the previous recipe and when serving you can just pull them apart.

Recipes for different fillings on following pages.

Stuffed Focaccia

Use the following method to fill, fold and bake the stuffed focaccia for all the recipes

Using a dough divider or scraper (see "Bread Baking Tools" section), divide the dough into 4 pieces after the fermentation (after step 3 in "Focaccia recipe, "Artisan Bread" section). Form the dough pieces into balls and cover them with plastic wrap and let them rest for 30 minutes. If the dough balls feel dry on the surface lightly spray them with oil or cover them with a damp cloth and mist the cloth lightly with water. Keeping the dough balls a bit humid will help them expand and stretch.

Stretch the dough balls into 7 by 12 inch rectangles about 1/4 inch thick. You can use a rolling pin but this dough recipe makes a very soft dough and it is very easy to stretch by hand. In case the dough is too soft and a bit too difficult to handle try reducing the water in the focaccia recipe by about 10 percent.

Place a quarter of the filling in the middle of the dough along the long side. Fold the dough like a letter enclosing the filling. Seal it well, cut it in half using a sharp knife and place the two pieces in an oiled baking pan with open ends touching. Lightly brush them or spray them with olive oil.

Do the same for the 3 other dough balls and bake in the middle to high rack for 30 minutes at 440 degrees Fahrenheit or until they're nicely browned. Rotate the pan 180 degrees 10 minutes before it finishes baking for equal browning. Cool for about 15 minutes before serving. See pictures on page 77.

Suggestion: If you like a thinner crust, stretch the dough into about 7 x 16 inch rectangles and after folding cut it into 3 pieces and proceed with the same instructions above.

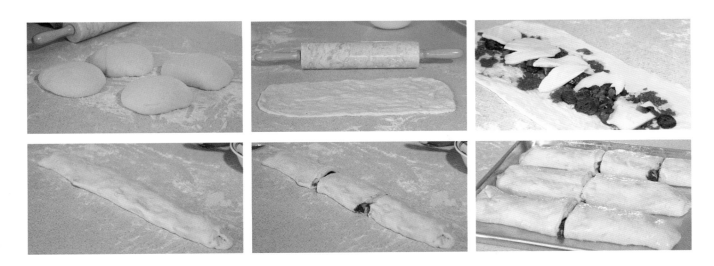

Stuffed Focaccia

Sun-Dried Tomato, Goat Cheese, Fresh Basil and Toasted Pine Nuts

1 cup sun dried tomato

1/2 cup toasted pine nuts

1 bunch fresh basil

1/2 lb crumbled goat cheese

2 lbs focaccia dough
(see "Artisan Bread" section)

Makes 8 stuffed focaccias

Spread about a quarter of the sun dried tomato in the middle of the stretched dough along the long side and top it with a quarter of the goat cheese, basil and pine nuts. Fold the dough like a letter, seal it well and cut it in half and place them in an oiled baking pan with open ends touching and lightly brush them with olive oil.

See page 79 for detailed instructions on how to stretch, fold and bake the focaccia.

Prosciutto, Mozzarella and Basil Pesto

1/2 cup basil pesto

1/2 lb prosciutto

1/2 lb Mozzarella

2 lbs focaccia dough
(see "Artisan Bread" section)

Makes 8 stuffed focaccias

Spread about a quarter of the basil pesto in the middle of the stretched dough along the long side and top it with a quarter of the mozzarella cheese and prosciutto. Fold the dough like a letter, seal it well and cut it in half and place them in an oiled baking pan with open ends touching and lightly brush them with olive oil.

See page 79 for detailed instructions on how to stretch, fold and bake the focaccia.

Greek Feta, Spinach and Nutmeg

1 lb frozen spinach

1/2 lb crumbled feta cheese

1/4 teaspoon ground nutmeg

2 lbs focaccia dough
(see "Artisan Bread" section)

Makes 8 stuffed focaccias

Mix the spinach, cheese and nutmeg together in a bowl and spread a quarter of it in the middle of the stretched dough along the long side. Fold the dough like a letter, seal it well and cut it in half and place it in an oiled baking pan with open ends touching and lightly brush them with olive oil.

See page 79 for detailed instructions on how to stretch, fold and bake the focaccia.

Note: You can also make panini grilled sandwiches with the recipes on this page using the same fillings. Use French or Ciabatta bread slices.

Stuffed Focaccia

Olive, Italian Herbs and Fresh Basil

1 cup olives cut in halves

2 teaspoons Italian herbs

1 bunch fresh chopped basil

2 lbs focaccia dough
(see "Artisan Bread" section)

Makes 8 stuffed focaccias

Mix the olives, herbs and basil together in a bowl and spread a quarter of it in the middle of the stretched dough along the long side. Fold the dough like a letter, seal it well and cut it in half and place them in an oiled baking pan with open ends touching and lightly brush them with olive oil.

See page 79 for detailed instructions on how to stretch, fold and bake the focaccia.

Olive, Onion and Fresh Mint

1 cup olives cut in halves

1 chopped onion

1 bunch chopped fresh mint

2 lbs focaccia dough
(see "Artisan Bread" section)

Makes 8 stuffed focaccias

Mix the olives, chopped onions and mint together in a bowl and spread a quarter of it in the middle of the stretched dough along the long side. Fold the dough like a letter, seal it well and cut it in half and place them in an oiled baking pan with open ends touching and lightly brush them with olive oil.

See page 79 for detailed instructions on how to stretch, fold and bake the focaccia.

Feta, Mozzarella, Cheddar, Parsley and Scallions

1/2 lb feta

1/2 lb mozzarella

1/2 lb cheddar

1/2 bunch chopped parsley

1/2 cup diced scallions

2 lbs focaccia dough
(see "Artisan Bread" section)

Makes 8 stuffed focaccias

Mix the cheese, scallions & parsley together in a bowl and spread a quarter of it in the middle of the stretched dough along the long side. Fold the dough like a letter, seal it well and cut it in half and place them in an oiled baking pan with open ends touching and lightly brush them with olive oil.

See page 79 for detailed instructions on how to stretch, fold and bake the focaccia.

Note: You can also make panini grilled sandwiches with this recipe using the same filling. Use French or Ciabatta bread slices.

Stuffed Focaccia

Salami, Mortadella, Prosciutto and Mozzarella Cheese

1/2 lb salami

1/2 lb mortadella

1/2 lb prosciutto

1/2 lb mozzarella

2 lbs focaccia dough
(see "Artisan Bread" section)

Makes 8 stuffed focaccias

Place a few slices of the cold cuts and top it with a quarter of the cheese in the middle of the stretched dough along the long side. Fold the dough like a letter, seal it well and cut it in half and place them in an oiled baking pan with open ends touching and lightly brush them with olive oil.

See page 79 for detailed instructions on how to stretch, fold and bake the focaccia.

Turkey and Smoked Cheddar

1 lb turkey

1/2 lb smoked cheddar

2 lbs focaccia dough
(see "Artisan Bread" section)

Makes 8 stuffed focaccias

Place a few slices of the turkey and top it with a quarter of the cheese in the middle of the stretched dough along the long side. Fold the dough like a letter, seal it well and cut it in half and place them in an oiled baking pan with open ends touching and lightly brush them with olive oil.

See page 79 for detailed instructions on how to stretch, fold and bake the focaccia.

Blue Cheese and Toasted Walnut

1 lb crumbled blue cheese

1 cup toasted crumbled walnuts

2 lbs focaccia dough
(see "Artisan Bread" section)

Makes 8 stuffed focaccias

Mix the cheese and walnuts in a bowl and spread a quarter of it in the middle of the stretched dough along the long side. Fold the dough like a letter, seal it well and cut in half and place them in an oiled baking pan with open ends touching and lightly brush them with olive oil.

See page 79 for detailed instructions on how to stretch, fold and bake the focaccia.

Note: You can also make panini grilled sandwiches with the recipes on this page using the same fillings. Use French or Ciabatta bread slices.

Feta,
Mozzarella,
Cheddar,
Parsley and
Scallions
Panini on Olive
Sourdough
Bread

Sun-Dried Tomatoes, Goat Cheese,
Toasted Pine Nuts and Basil Panini on Ciabatta

Toast the pine nuts in a toaster for few minutes until they brown.

Tuna Melt Panini on Rye Bread

Rye bread is usually dense because rye flour is low in gluten so the dough does not rise very much. This rye bread is made with 60% whole rye flour.

3 small cans tuna

4 slices cheddar cheese

1/4 cup diced scallions

1/3 cup mayonnaise

Makes 4 sandwiches

Stuffed Focaccia

Spinach, Onion, Lemon Juice and Sumac

This one is a Middle Eastern Roll called "Spinach Fatayer". Typically it is shaped into triangle rolls but making it into focaccia will taste the same and is easier to make.

1 1/2 lbs frozen or fresh chopped spinach

2 chopped onions

2 tablespoons sumac

1/2 teaspoon salt

Juice of 2 lemons

1 tablespoon olive oil

2 lbs focaccia dough (see "Artisan Bread" section)

Makes 8 stuffed focaccias

Wash the spinach and squeeze the water out, add the rest of the ingredients and mix together in a bowl. Spread a quarter of the filling in the middle of the stretched dough along the long side. Fold the dough like a letter, seal it well and cut in half and place them in an oiled baking pan with open ends touching and lightly brush them with olive oil.

See page 79 for detailed instructions on how to stretch, fold and bake the focaccia.

Option: You can add 3 to 4 tablespoons toasted pine nuts to the filling.

Sumac can be ordered online but if you can't find it you can omit it. It resembles a coarse paprika like powder but it is not a spice, it is made out of crushed red sumac berries that grow in clusters on trees and has a tangy flavor.

Ground Beef, Onion, Toasted Pine Nuts and Spices

2 lbs ground beef

2 chopped onions

1/2 teaspoon cinnamon

1/2 teaspoon allspice or black pepper

3/4 teaspoon salt

2 tablespoons sumac (optional)

1/2 cup toasted pine nuts

3 tablespoons vegetable oil

2 lbs focaccia dough (see "Artisan Bread" section)

Makes 8 stuffed focaccias

Heat oil in a pan, add chopped onion and sauté few minutes until they soften. Add ground beef, salt, cinnamon and allspice and cook until well done. Transfer to a bowl, add sumac, toasted pine nuts and mix together. Spread a quarter of the mix in the middle of the stretched dough along the long side. Fold the dough like a letter, seal it well and cut it in half and place them in an oiled baking pan with open ends touching and lightly brush them with olive oil.

See page 79 for detailed instructions on how to stretch, fold and bake the focaccia.

Suggestion: You can also add 2 fresh chopped tomatoes to the mixture.

Note: These are typically Middle Eastern rolls shaped into small half moons. They also make them into pizzas using the tomatoes, a tablespoon of tomato paste and finely chopped green chili pepper if you like it hot.

Prosciutto and Mozzarella Mini Focaccia

Spreads & Dips

Wasabe Mayonnaise

Wasabe comes in a tube already made or as a powder. If using the powder add few drops of water to a teaspoon of wasabe and mix into a paste. Whisk the wasabe into the mayonnaise with a fork.

1 teaspoon wasabe

1/3 cup mayonnaise

Roasted Garlic Mayonnaise

Place the garlic cloves on an aluminum foil, drizzle a bit of olive oil, enclose and roast them in the oven for about 25 minutes at 375 degrees Fahrenheit. Let cool then squeeze the garlic out of the skin by pinching one end and mash it into the mayonnaise with a fork. Place it in the fridge for 30 minutes to chill and serve.

Option: You can add a tablespoon of chopped parsley to the mayonnaise for more texture & flavor.

4 garlic cloves skin on

1/3 cup mayonnaise

1 teaspoon olive oil

Pickled Turnip

Cut out the top and bottom of the turnips and beet, cut them in 1/2 inch wedges or slices, wash them and place them in a glass jar. Fill the jar with 1/4 white vinegar and 3/4 water adding the salt and close the jar with a lid. The turnips will be ready to eat in about 10 days. When using them in a sandwich cut the wedges in 1/4 inch strips.

The beet is used only to give the turnips a deep red color.

2 lbs turnips

1 beet

1/2 cup white vinegar

1 1/2 cups water

2 teaspoons salt

Garlic Spread (Toum)

Crush the garlic with salt and lemon juice using a blender. Lightly drizzle some of the oil and blend for few seconds. Drizzle again some oil and blend again for few seconds. Repeat the process of drizzling and blending until you get a white thick consistency that resembles mayonnaise. If you have used all the oil and the consistency is still watery and not thick enough you can add a tablespoon of mayonnaise and mix it with a spoon. You can also boil a cup of water in a saucepan, add 2 tablespoons cornstarch and let it cool to a jello like consistency. Scoop 2 tablespoons of that consistency and blend it for few seconds with the garlic mixture to thicken it.

1 whole bulb garlic (about 12 cloves)

2 tablespoons lemon juice or white vinegar

1/2 teaspoon salt

1 cup vegetable oil

Tahini Sauce

Tahini is ground sesame that comes in jars available at many super markets or Middle Eastern stores. To make it into sauce simply add water and lemon juice, mix it well and serve. It is served with falafel, shawarma and many Middle Eastern dishes.

1/2 cup tahini

3/4 cup water

Juice of 2 lemons

Hummus

Soak the garbanzo beans and baking soda in water overnight. Drain the water and place the beans in a cooking pot, cover with water and cook on high heat until it starts boiling and a white foam appears on top. Lower the heat to medium low, remove the foam with a spoon and cook for about an hour and a half until the beans are soft.

Drain the water, place the beans in a blender and blend until somewhat smooth. Mash the garlic and add it to the beans with the lemon juice, salt, tahini and blend them again until very smooth.
Garnish the hummus plate with paprika, olive oil and few whole cooked beans & parsley.

Suggestion: After blending the beans set aside 3 tablespoons before adding the lemon juice and tahini. If the hummus is too watery add the 3 tablespoons of beans that you set aside to thicken the consistency. If the hummus is too thick add few tablespoons of water.

1 1/2 cups garbanzo beans

1/2 teaspoon baking soda

5 cloves garlic

1 1/4 teaspoons salt

1/2 cup lemon juice

1/3 cup tahini

Tartar Sauce

Mix all ingredients in a bowl and chill in the fridge for 30 minutes and serve.

1/2 cup mayonnaise

1 tablespoon minced dill pickle or fresh dill

1 tablespoon finely chopped or grated onion

1 tablespoon chopped capers

1 tablespoon lemon juice

Salt & pepper to taste

Tzatziki

Peel the cucumber, cut it in half lengthwise and remove the seeds with a spoon and coarsely grate it. Squeeze the grated cucumber with your hand to remove excess water and dry it with a cloth. Finely grate the garlic and mix all ingredients in a bowl with a fork. Chill the dip in the fridge for few hours to help the yogurt absorb the flavor of the garlic. It is a good idea to prepare this dip a day before you serve it to obtain full flavor.

1 small cucumber

3 garlic cloves

1 tablespoon wine vinegar

2 cups Greek style plain yogurt

2 tablespoons extra virgin olive oil

1/2 tablespoon chopped dill leaves

Bread Baking Tools

Bowl, measuring
cups & spoons

Baking pan, loaf pan, cotton cloth

Sprayer, liquid measuring cup,
scraper (or dough divider), spatula

Rolling pin

Serrated knife or blade for
scoring dough. Scale (optional)
for measuring by weight.
Thermometer (optional) to
measure oven temperature

Long wood board for
transferring baguettes from
couche.

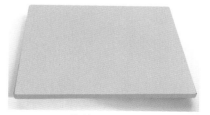

Baking stone

Electric mixer (optional)
if not kneading by hand

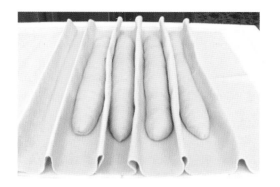

Baker's couche is a canvas cloth made with untreated natural fiber used to proof (ferment) the dough. The rough surface absorbs the extra moisture in the dough giving the bread a thick crispy crust which is a characteristic of French bread. It is also sturdy enough to hold a round shape to create a dividing wall between the loaves to prevent them from sticking to each other. You will still get acceptable results without it but if you want to perfect your bread like the French do and get a nice thick crust, you can buy it online at: *Daniel's Rustic Bread:* www.danielsrusticbread.com

Baskets are also used with the couche to proof round and oval loaves to help keep the round shape of the loaves. If you don't have a basket proof on a flat surface and fold the couche around the loaf.

Super Peel gently lifts and moves the most delicate or sticky dough from prep area to pan or oven stone. Use for freeform breads, pizzas, pies, pastry... The peel provides a large dough carrying surface; and dough does not stick to the lightly floured pastry cloth which wraps around the peel creating a small hand-held conveyor belt, which has amazing dough transferring and handling properties. To order the Super Peel or see an online video on how it works log on to: www.superpeel.com or www.danielsrusticbread.com

Index

Bread Recipes

Sandwiches by Bread Type

About The Author

Sam Sidawi started researching and practicing artisan bread making In 1999 when he was living in California. In 2005 he published his first instructional DVD on how to make baguettes and traditional French bread. Today he has ten DVD titles featuring different kinds of artisan bread available online at: Daniel's Rustic Bread - www.danielsrusticbread.com. Sam presently lives in Montreal Canada.

DVD titles published by Daniel's Rustic Bread:

Baguettes & Traditional French Bread
French Country Bread (Pain de campagne)
French Sourdough Bread (Pain au levain)
Ciabatta & Rustic Italian Bread
Traditional & Stuffed Italian Bread
Pizza & Calzones
Whole Grain, Multi-Grain & Seeds
Mediterranean Delights
Sweet Bread
Croissant & Variations